Alexander Barrett

This first edition was published November 10, 2015

First printing of 3,000 copies. Distributed by **Legato/Perseus**

ISBN 978-1-62106-903-4

This book was printed on post-consumer paper in the United States.

MicrocosmPublishing.com

Welcome to

上海

SHÀNG HǍI

"Upon-the-Sea"

By the time I landed, it was the future.

The flight was only eleven hours long, but thanks to the international date line, we arrived twenty hours after we departed. So it was really only nine hours in the future, but those nine hours must have made all the difference.

In my jet-lagged mind, time was meaningless. It was dark, so I assumed it was night. I found my driver. He grabbed my bags and took off toward the parking lot. I had to run to keep up. It was only after he slammed the door behind me that I realized I had gotten into a car with a stranger whose language I did not speak. And I was in a country I'd never been to before. And I had no idea where we were going. And I could barely keep my eyes open.

The road was empty. Fields of twinkling lights. Rows upon rows of gigantic, darkened apartment blocks silhouetted against the light pollution. Skyscrapers covered with millions of LEDs putting on a show for no one in particular. The elevated roads glowed blue, a system of highways made of pure light. Later, I'd learn that this effect is created by a string of well-placed party lights underneath the road, but, for now, I was in the movie *Bladerunner*.

At some point, I fell asleep. When I woke, the car was stopped and the driver was yelling at me. My door was open. My bags were on the sidewalk. I pulled myself together, got out of the car, and he drove away. No signs and no lights, I stood at the entrance of a lane. The name of my hotel was buried somewhere in my phone, but I didn't even have the cell service to find it.

Then, in the darkness, I heard quick footsteps. A voice said:

"Hello. Hello. Alexander. Hello. Hello."

He came into the light for a split second, grabbed my belongings, and made off down the lane. I followed as fast as I could. Before I knew it, we were upstairs; he dropped my bags and made sure to show me the bathroom, complete with Hello Kitty shower curtain. I nodded in approval, he disappeared.

I found a bed and climbed into it.

Then I lived in Shanghai.

That was over a year ago.

Since then, I've seen, heard, smelled, and learned a lot. You'll find all of it collected here.

This is a guidebook, but it won't tell you where to eat or what to see. It'll tell you how it is. These are the stories I tell when I go home. When people ask me "So, what's it like to live in Shanghai?"

This is what the most common metropolitan experience in the world means to me.

This is Shanghai.

Jian Bing

The night before I left for Shanghai, I was at a bar in Portland, Oregon. My friend Jess had just come back from China and she was giving me some pointers. When it was time to go, she reached into her pocket, took out a handful of coins, and put them into my hand.

She told me that when I woke up on my first day, I should walk down the street until I find a food item that kind of looks like a pancake, but with other stuff in it.

When I asked her what the other stuff was, she told me to "just eat it."

I woke up in Shanghai completely confused with six RMB in coin to my name. That's a little under one U.S. dollar. Shanghai was different in the light. Quieter and more green than I had expected. I didn't know that I was in the heart of the Former French Concession, but we'll talk about that later.

My confusion quickly turned to hunger and I knew that the only thing I could do was find the thing that Jess had told me about, so I put on pants and walked out the door.

I didn't really know what I was looking for, but half a block later, I was staring at something that kind of looked like a pancake, but with other stuff in it.

I'd find out later that it's called Jian Bing.

There was a man standing behind a big, circular cooking surface in the entryway of a closed restaurant. I held up one finger. He held up four fingers. When I put four coins in his coin tray, I had no idea that I was about to get breakfast and a show.

Here's his performance, step by step.

1. He threw a scoop of batter onto the cooking surface and spread it into a circle with some kind of culinary trowel.

2. Immediately, he cracked an egg and broke it up over the surface.

3. He tossed a handful of chopped spring onions on there.

4. He used a trowel to separate the whole thing from the cooking surface and fold it in half.

5. He grabbed a big spoon and spread a generous scoop of the brownest sauce imaginable all over the place.

6. Chili sauce is optional. He pointed at it, I nodded, then he incorporated it into the brown area.

7. He reached into a trash bag behind him and pulled out a big piece of fried something. He threw it in the middle and broke it up with the trowel.

8. More folding. So much folding.

9. By this point, I had not taken a small plastic bag from the condiment area and was not holding it open to accept the Jian Bing, so he yelled at me.

10. He repeated the process immediately because there were and always are a million people in his line.

When the show was over, I took my little plastic breakfast bag back to my room and ate the first real Chinese food of my life.

My mouth was happy.

My stomach, not so much.

4 Yuan

4 RMB

4 QUAI

People Everywhere

When I tell people I live in a city of twenty-four million people, I don't think they really get it. They say "Wow. I can't imagine." And they're right, they can't.

But I really can't either. Numbers are different here.

I once met a woman who said she was from a small town outside the city. I asked how many people lived there. She said five million.

That's not a small town, that's multiple Chicagos.

I don't think I've ever seen twenty-four million of anything. It's impossible to picture. So I started thinking about it differently. What does being around 23,999,999 other people feel like on a day to day basis?

Well, when you walk down the street, you are going to bump into people. You'll catch an elbow here, a hip check there. Sometimes, for a split second, your entire body will be touching another person. And it won't be because they're angry or they've become intensely attracted to you all of a sudden.

It's only because the space in which you currently exist has been overbooked.

There are so many people that somebody's elbow has to be in the same space as your stomach right now or else Shanghai will burst.

If this old woman cannot lean on your back, a man on the edge of a dock will be pushed out to sea.

And when you finally get through this sea of humanity, make it into your apartment, and manage to shut the door without seriously injuring anyone, the sea will still be there. Pressed up against your door. Just smoking, talking, living their lives, waiting for a little more space to open up.

This is what it means to live in the equivalent of three New York Cities piled on top of each other.

Personal space does not exist. It is a myth. A legend from the ancient times. When people get a little too close for comfort, the residents of Shanghai won't give you an "excuse me;" they'll simply walk on. They won't expect one from you, either, so don't worry about it. The moment is over as soon as it happens. You can get upset all you like but it won't do any good. It's nobody's fault; it's just the nature of this city.

So you'd better get over it quick because a baby was just born which means your butt is about to share some space with someone else's.

Sidewalk Art

The sidewalks in Shanghai are made of loose bricks packed with sand. They're made this way because there are pipes underneath. The **pipe guys** need to get to those pipes more often than you'd think. So instead of breaking out a jackhammer, all they have to do is pick up some bricks, dig up some sand, and there they are.

When the **brick guys** install a new sidewalk, its bricks can be colored and laid out in beautiful, well-designed patterns, or they can be a regular dark grey and placed in a grid. When they're dark grey, another team of workers will create bike-parking areas. A bike parking area consists of a large painted white box with a bicycle icon stenciled in the center. When all these guys are finished with their work, the red tape is removed and the public is free to walk on their perfect new sidewalks.

Eventually, though, there will be a pipe problem. And the pipe guys will need to get to the pipes. So they pick up the bricks, dig up the sand, do their stuff, and that's when we find out why pipe guys are pipe guys and brick guys are brick guys.

When the pipe guys replace the bricks, it's very clear that no one has been given the task of keeping track of which brick goes where. All the bricks are the same shape and they can go anywhere. So obviously, the pipe guys put any brick anywhere.

Which means that every single brick returns to the wrong place. And patterns are patterns no more.

At first look, it's a garbled mess. But when you live with it-and you will live with it because no one is going to put everything right again-it becomes part of the city's aesthetic.

Eventually, they become metaphors for the city itself. Everything is just a little off. It's not working perfectly and nobody seems to care.

But these "off" things are what gives Shanghai its personality. These are the reasons you are here. They are things that are worth experiencing because they don't happen wherever you come from.

When you are able to realize this, those stenciled bicycles become breathtaking Dadaist representations of bicycles. And the once-perfectly-executed concrete configurations become exercises in Abstract Expressionism.

Nothing is the way it should be, and that's the most beautiful thing of all.

Spitting

Shanghai has agreed as a city upon a "better out than in" policy. As a Westerner fresh off the boat, it can be a very tall cultural barrier to climb.

Everywhere you go, you'll hear and see that patriotic salute to internal health: "Hhhhhhchchchch, ptoo!"

And when I say "everywhere," I mean "everywhere."

Obviously, it's on the street and in the bathroom. But less obviously, it's on the train, it's on the plane, it's at the dinner table, it's at the breakfast stall both in front of and behind the counter. It's actually outside my door right now as I type this at ten o'clock on a Friday night. It's like someone is standing directly outside my apartment for the express purpose of grossing me out.

And this is twenty-four hours a day. Sometimes I'll wake up in the middle of the night and just as I start to enjoy a rare silent moment, I'll hear a throat rattle rolling somewhere in the darkness.

A word of warning: with all this spit flying around, it's only a matter of time before some lands on you. When that happens, just keep in mind that no one is trying to spit on you. It's just that they're not trying all that hard to not.

You can complain all you want, but after a while, when the pollution really sets up shop in your lungs, you'll wake up with a mouthful of slime and think: "Ugh, that came from my body?! I'd like it out immediately please!"

Then you hock up something gross and join the party.

Welcome.

Laowai

I was exploring on the outskirts of the city when I found a park with a big hill in the middle.

I was sweating when I reached the top. There didn't seem to be anyone around. All I could see was a small pagoda at the end of the path.

As I got closer, an elderly man walked slowly out of the shadows. Very slowly. His cane was doing most of the work. I had no idea how he'd gotten to the top of this hill all by himself. Then I started to think that there was some kind of ancient Chinese knowledge I could glean from this man.

We locked eyes. And as he passed he yelled:

"NI HAO, LAOWAI!"

Basically, what he meant was "Hey, white boy!" Then he started laughing hysterically. And then I laughed because he is right; Laowais are ridiculous.

Laowai means "foreigner." If you're here and you aren't Chinese, you are one. And you will be called one. It's also a collective term used to describe the entire expatriat community.

The only other way I've heard it used is when locals are talking about prices.

I once tried to brag that I only paid ten RMB for a bootleg DVD to a local. She replied: "ten RMB!? That's Laowai Price. I get them for five." I nodded, agreed that she was better than me, and fought the urge to say:

"Congratulations for saving 80 cents."

I am able to declare proudly that I am a Laowai. And if my role here is to be the butt of jokes for elderly Shanghainese men with above-average leg strength, I'm totally fine with it.

the Former French Concession

In 1849, the French Consul to Shanghai wanted to set up an official French settlement. He asked the city and the city was cool with it, so the French Concession was born.

Over the years, it's gone through all kinds of changes. The biggest one is that it's not really the French Concession anymore, it's "the Former French Concession." But after all this time, it is still known as the place where all the white people live.

Located in the heart of Puxi, which is the the half of the city west of the Huangpu River, the French Concession is home to tree-lined streets, beautiful late-nineteenth and early-twentieth-century architecture, and most of the coffee shops.

It's pleasant.

Pleasancy is a hard thing to find in Shanghai. I feel like a real spoiled Laowai saying it, but when you're not from here it's tough to be comfortable. That's why a lot of Western companies set up their Chinese headquarters in the French Concession, and that's why all the Laowais are here.

This became very clear to me on one of my first nights in the city.

My new friends had invited me to Yongkang Road for a drink. They said it was a block of bars with outdoor seating. When I arrived, I could have sworn I was anywhere other than Asia. Wall to wall foreigners drinking and speaking every language other than Mandarin.

It was almost disappointing. I'd come here to be surrounded by the unknown and I ended up with a can of Budweiser.

But if you have that feeling, it will go away when you realize that the expat community is a great source of support. And you're in it as soon as you get off the plane.

Most of my new friends came from the office. The rest were people who used to work at the office, significant others of people who work at the office, and significant others of people who used to work at the office. They took me under their wings from day one. It was only months later I realized they were getting just as much out of the deal as I was. There's nothing like some fresh meat to liven up your social circle.

So you mix and you mingle and suddenly you realize that you don't have to be the only stranger in a strange land. You can be weirded out by Shanghai together. And you can definitely discover that it's legal to drink in public together.

And if things ever get too intense and you need some good old-fashioned comfort, you can grab your crew of Laowais and walk over to Fortune Cookie on Changshu Road for some American-style Chinese food. It's Chinese food that you would never find in China.

The fact that this restaurant can remain in business shows you just how robust the expat community has become. Because Chinese people are not eating this food. Many have made fun of me for going.

To them I say: "Hey, Tso was *your* General. If you don't like his chicken, it's not my problem."

the Lane House

When looking for an apartment in Shanghai, you have two options: You can either get a cookie-cutter box in a high rise or you can delve into one of the city's intricate lane systems. They're called "longtang." These are interconnected alleyways filled with houses, small apartment buildings, and businesses.

The longtang are what gives Shanghai pretty much all of its charm. They started popping up at the turn of the last century and when you step into one you can really feel it. There's laundry hanging all around, outdoor sinks filled with pots, fish drying, chickens hanging, and chamber pots left out from the night before. And quarters are very tight. But after spending all day in the big city, a longtang feels like a little architectural hug.

I chose a lane house. But before I did, there were people who warned me against them. They said that it would be crowded. And that there would be no insulation so I'd be hot in the summer and cold in the winter. And that the walls would be thin. And that everything would always break. And they were right.

To get to my apartment, I have to go through the foyer, which has become a sea of rusting bicycles. There are no windows and only one dim bulb flickering fifteen feet above my head so, whatever the hour, I have to go through that maze in the dark. If I make it out alive, I go through the first of three semi-public kitchens I'll traverse on my journey.

Then up the stairs. The sound-activated lights are a little hard of hearing, so I usually use my phone to light my way. If you didn't know where you were going at this point, you'd swear you were in a condemned building. But then you'd go through the second and third kitchen and you would realize that it is in fact inhabited.

If my neighbor across the hall is cooking, I'm home free. If my next-door neighbor is cooking, he will be using so much chili that all the air on the third floor will turn into pepper gas. I cover my face with my shirt, take out my keys, and sprint into my apartment.

Even with the door closed, I can hear the ear-splitting sizzle of oil hitting the pan. There is no "low" on Chinese stove tops. Only "hot" and "charred." I can hear it because they were right: the walls are thin. There's a baby crying, the jazz vocalist who lives upstairs is practicing her craft, there's a woman somewhere who's angry at someone, and there's a cat who isn't getting something that it thinks it needs.

And it's cold in here because they were right: there is no insulation. Right now it's winter and my heat is broken because they were right: everything always breaks. When it's time for bed, I'll take a hot shower and lay all the clothes I can't fit on my body on top of my blankets.

But I won't really care because this is Shanghai and I came here to live in Shanghai, not in an apartment building that could be anywhere else in the world.

Someday soon the high rises will win the city. The longtang are disappearing in the name of progress. It's not uncommon to go for a walk and come across a flattened block of lane houses. Just a big field of bricks waiting to be something big and square and new.

I've stood in the middle of one of those fields. Only this one wasn't fully torn down. There were a few halves of houses left. And people were living in them, waiting to have their space compensated with a high rise apartment of equal size.

From that field, I had a perfect view of Shanghai Tower, still under construction. The second-tallest building in the world getting even taller, and a little boy climbing up a pile of rocks that used to be somebody's home. I went back to my apartment, sat on my couch, and decided to enjoy my longtang while it's still in one piece.

Well, kind of in one piece, anyway. The knob just fell off my bathroom door.

WHEN IN SHANGHAI, VISIT

Lane

22

Ayi

In Mandarin, "Ayi" means "Auntie." It's a word you can use to address any older woman.

But it's also a term used for a woman you can hire to do things around your home. Kind of like a maid, but different.

When I showed up in Shanghai, my friends told me to get an Ayi. I thought it was too extravagant. I couldn't imagine that I'd have much for her to do anyway. Then, the HR department at work encouraged me to hire one to support the local economy.

So I have an Ayi. Her name is Shao. And she is not really a maid. She is a grandmother-for-hire.

Shao's English and my Mandarin are, well, terrible is a strong word, but let's go with it anyway. We communicate by my pointing at things and her not really knowing what I mean. So I just leave, and when I get home the thing I wanted her to do is magically done anyway.

She cleans my apartment, does my dishes, makes my bed, pays my bills, buys me food, and cleans my sneakers. I didn't even know sneakers could be cleaned. At this point I'm just bragging, but this is a beautiful part of living in Shanghai.

I really have to work hard to keep my guilt out of the way of our relationship. Most mornings before she comes, I find myself in a mad rush of picking up and straightening everything so I won't seem like a terrible person. But I really don't have to worry, because there's no judgment. She shows up with a smile and never complains.

Actually, I guess she could be complaining about me behind my back, but even if I overheard it I wouldn't be able to understand, so it's totally fine.

Sometimes when I get homesick, I just think about what my life was like before I had an Ayi. What life was like when I put dishes in the sink and they didn't disappear the next day. Terrible.

In the end, I'm really just setting myself up for disappointment. Because I know I'll go home someday. And when I do, Shao won't be there to take care of me.

Pajamas

In Shanghai, pajamas are a way of life. If you're not going into work or out to dinner, they are considered appropriate attire. Children wear them in the lane, twenty-somethings wear them down to the noodle shop, middle aged people wear them while chatting with friends or playing mahjong, and the elderly wear them everywhere, all the time.

These aren't your everyday PJs. Wearing a pair is like wearing a suit made out of quilts. And they usually feature very loud patterns. The visual equivalent of a strobe light. I once saw an old man walking down the street in a full-body Mondrian painting made out polar fleece. I gave him a big thumbs up and he was utterly confused.

Even though they're crazy comfortable, there's a lot more happening when you throw on a pair and hit the town. First, you're saying to everyone around you that you have the money to spend on an extravagant pair of pajamas. They're not very expensive, but at a few hundred RMB, they're not cheap either. Second, you're saying that yours is a life of leisure. You have no time or need for pants. You've got a lot of sitting around to do.

Pajamas have become a status symbol.

And they work, too. One day while I was standing at a crosswalk, a scooter pulled in front of me. Riding side saddle on the back was a man wearing only pajama bottoms and flip flops. He was eating a popsicle and rocking his legs back and forth as his friend drove. This was a man who knew who he was. This was a man who knew exactly what he wanted out of life.

I wanted to chase after him.

I wanted to scream:

"SIR, PLEASE TELL ME YOUR SECRET!"

Little Friends Everywhere

I took a ride on the back of my friend Yaya's scooter. She had just moved back to Shanghai after a few years in Portland and her first goal was to get rid of her gigantic rice cooker. That's where I came in. I was about to buy a gigantic rice cooker. As soon as we pulled into the parking lot, a puppy came bounding out of a nearby shed, landed on my foot, and sat, looking up at me

I had to pick him up. Yaya took the top picture you see here. Then I put him down and we went inside to get the rice cooker. It was a really big rice cooker, but we were sure I could carry it on the back of the scooter all the way home.

When we went back outside, the puppy was still next to the bike, waiting for us.

I looked at the puppy. I looked at my big, puppy-sized rice cooker, the perfect way to transport a puppy on the back of a scooter. Then I thought about my serious allergy to puppies. Then I started the process again. It went on for a good minute.

In the end, the allergies won. I had to leave my new little friend. My heart was broken. But I didn't know that these little friends would be a regular occurrence.

Listen, there's nothing sadder than a poorly controlled pet population.

However, in Shanghai, that means every once in a while, you'll be walking down the street and SURPRISE! a puppy wants to be your friend. Or HI THERE! a collection of kittens just wants to see what you're up to.

And you can pick them up or leave them to go about their business and hope it all goes well.

They'll grow up. Kittens will join the rest of the cats in the city's public park system, where felines rule supreme. And the puppies will fall into the ranks of the wild dog population, creating new generations of lovable tramps who beg for food and always get it.

the People's Puppy

The idea of the pet dog is still pretty new to China, but this city has really started to embrace it.

However, it seems that when the catalog of dogs hit the doorsteps of Shanghai, the entire city opened it to the first page, saw a brown miniature poodle, and said in unison:

"Yep, that's a dog. It's cute. We'll take it."

Then, they all closed the catalog and threw it in the trash, never to be looked at again.

Yes, there are other dogs here, but the proliferation of that tiny brown fluffball is staggering. They are everywhere.

If you think about it, it's a pretty smart move. They're even-tempered, quiet, hypoallergenic; they look great in a sweater, and they fit easily into your handbag or bicycle basket.

They should really start thinking about putting these little guys on the flag.

"the Weather"

In the Summer of 2013, my sister announced that she and her family were moving to China. I'd never thought about going to China before but I was freelancing at the time and figured I could get a company to fly me out so I could visit her for free. A few months later, I had a job and a ticket.

I asked my sister if she wanted anything from home. She said:

"Bring masks."

The Air Quality Index (AQI) is a number that lets us know exactly how much pollution is in our lungs right now. And exactly how disgusting we currently feel.

People refer to it as "The Weather."

The AQI takes all kinds of amounts of particulates of varying sizes and gives us a nice, round number to be terrified of.

Here's how I like to break it down:

My hometown is Montpelier, VT. The AQI in Montpelier, VT hovers around zero.

For years, I lived in Los Angeles, CA. The AQI in Los Angeles, CA as I'm writing this is 78.

One day in my second week in Shanghai, I woke up to an AQI of over 300. I went outside, assuming this was a normal, everyday number. I felt like I was eating the air. By the time I got to work, it had hit 400. My coworkers told me they'd never seen it so high. That's when I started getting scared.

An email from the HR department followed. They'd been to every pharmacy trying to find surgical masks for everyone, but they were all sold out. Instead, they'd purchased and prepared a few pounds of pears, which were available in the kitchen if anyone needed a snack.

They also mentioned that the office was in no way air-tight, so the AQI inside was just as bad as the AQI outside. So if we didn't have too much work, we could go home to our apartments where we would be breathing the same air, but at least we'd be doing it on a couch.

I had a meeting after lunch, so going home wasn't an option. When I walked into the meeting room, the projector was on. I could see the projector's beam reach all the way to the screen, a perfect triangle of light reflecting off every particulate. That's when the AQI passed 500 and quickly went off the charts.

That's also when I went home and assumed the fetal position under my covers for the rest of the day.

In the morning, we learned that the day before had been the first really cold day of winter in Northern China. Everyone had turned on their heat at the same time, which triggered all the coal plants to start pumping out that famous Shanghai pollution.

That day, I bought the most heavy-duty respirator I could find. All black neoprene. It makes me look like

Darth Vader at the end of *Return of the Jedi*. You know that moment when he finally removes his mask, ensuring his death?

That's how I live now.

Everyone knows there are long-term effects of hanging out in polluted air all day every day. If you live here, it's best to wear a mask, put an air filter or five in your apartment, and try your best to not think about it.

But it seems like people don't know about the short-term effects. When the AQI gets to around 200, you can feel it in your body.

You'll cough, your nose will run, you'll have some extra gunk in the back of your throat, you'll get headaches, and most surprisingly, you'll get very, very sleepy.

When the air is bad, everyone turns into a cranky baby.

Meetings get mean, family dinners get confrontational, first dates go NOWHERE. What a nightmare.

If you're feeling extra cranky, it's best to take a step back, check the AQI app on your phone, and if it's high, put on your mask, go home and lay down. If it's low, you have other problems to worry about.

But you also can't focus on the AQI. Living in fear of "The Weather" doesn't lead to a happy Shanghai experience. It only makes you want to leave. If the air is only kind of bad, you really have to take off the mask and accept the city into your lungs before you accept it into your heart.

AQI	RESPONSE
100	you're fine
150	wear a mask
200	freak out
300	FREAK OUT!
400	FREAK OUT!
500	FREAK OUT!

the Beauty of a High AQI

Shanghai's pollution is, for the most part, awful. But there's one thing that almost, not really, but kind of, makes it okay:

Pollution is the ultimate diffusion.

You walk out of the house in the morning and all of a sudden you're bathed in perfect, magical light. So soft, so warm. All you have to do is grab anyone and ask them to take a picture of you. No matter what camera they use, you'll look like a million RMB.

When the pollution is just right, it's twilight all day long. It's a painting of the city, not the real thing. It's beautiful, but you can only live in it for so long.

Eventually, you'll look to the sky and think: "Wait, how am I able to stare directly at the sun? Why don't my eyes hurt? Isn't this supposed to be bad for me? Oh yeah, there's a couple miles of dust in between us. I should go inside and never come out again.

As I write this, the AQI has hit 300. It's nighttime. And the light from the LEDs of nearby skyscrapers is captured in the haze. My apartment is surrounded by blue and pink clouds.

I no longer live on Earth. Thanks, pollution.

the Weather

Shanghai's actual weather is pretty temperate, though it can get hot in the summer. But that's okay, because Shanghainese men have developed the perfect technique to beat the heat. And it only takes one step: roll up your shirt.

The art of the
SHANGHAINESE
T-SHIRT ROLL

25°-30°

30°-35°

NIPS →

35° and above

your guide to SHANGHAI

Jin Mao Tower

The Art Deco-iest.

the Pearl Tower

Finished in 1994, but straight out of a 1950s Sci-Fi movie.

SKYSCRAPERS

Shanghai World Financial Center

People called it "The Bottle Opener" because look at it.

Shanghai Tower

Too big.

Eat Dangerously

I lay down on the paper sheet in the examination room, writhing in pain with my third case of food poisoning.

"Sanitation is not China's highest priority," my doctor said. "You should be careful what you eat." And I agreed, promising to never eat whatever I had eaten again and he gave me some nice pills and I left.

But as I was leaving, I realized that this is not a problem with China. This is a problem with my stomach. My stomach is a wimp. You don't see Chinese people doubled over in their bathrooms every other week. You don't see them checking the grill for bacteria when they pick up a skewer of street meat. And you don't see them care if the animal that skewer came from was butchered on the very sidewalk where they are currently standing.

I envy Shanghai's strong stomachs. That's why I'm trying to develop one of my own.

If you are a Westerner who comes to Shanghai for an extended period of time, you are going to get sick. There's no way around it. You have to eat and you'll never know where the bug will come from. So instead of stressing out about it, just accept the fact that you are going to barf and it's going to be awful, but you'll live.

Don't think, just eat.

Eat with reckless abandon. Invite the bugs into your life. Really work out that stomach. Because someday, you'll go home and everything you put in your mouth will be sterilized. Sure, it may not taste good, but it'll be safe.

That's when you'll realize that after being in China, no meal can be truly great without a sense of danger.

a Winter Wonderland

When you walk down a street filled with street food vendors, your feet will eventually land in a puddle of something that seems like water but quickly reveals itself to be something very, very different.

Something you probably shouldn't inquire about. Something rendered. Something that was probably cute once, but not so cute now that your feet are covered in it.

You'll know when it happens because you'll take a step and plant your foot, but you'll keep moving. You'll be sliding over the sidewalk. When you've finally come to a stop a few feet later, you have two options:

1. Get super grossed out, find the nearest trashcan, ditch your shoes, run home barefoot, and spend the rest of the day in the tub, scrubbing your feet.

or

2. Pull it together, pretend you're on a picturesque lake in the dead of winter, and skate. Skate with all your might. Work on your form, figure, or speed; it doesn't matter.

One coating should get you about half a block away from the food stalls and take most the gunk off your shoes in the process.

Note: In summer, substitute roller skating. In hot weather, you'll probably go a lot farther, as there are far more different kinds of slippery substances all over the ground.

Don't inquire about those, either.

Elderly Public Exercise

If you're out for a stroll at dawn, or on your way to work, or heading to lunch, or heading home from work, or going out for a late dinner, you'll see them.

The old people of Shanghai are outdoors and they are working out.

Very, very slowly.

If you are an old person who's looking to do some exercise, you have a lot options to choose from. Let's go through them now.

Morning

In the early morning, you'll find a Tai Chi group in your local park mellowing out with their flowing movements and woodwind music. Some will be practicing with swords. They'll try to make eye contact with you as if to say, "Check out my sword. Aren't I very cool for an old person?" They'll be right.

Maybe a more modern regimen is right for you. If so, just head to the courtyard of your apartment complex. There, you'll find your peers going crazy on the most colorful exercise equipment you will have ever seen. They are a public service. It seems like there are more of these exercise areas for the elderly than there are playgrounds. No, these devices don't offer any resistance, but you'll be twisting, turning, swinging, and getting that blood flowing for the day. Also, you'll be wearing your pajamas. Because aren't you always?

Tai Chi and outdoor "gyms" can be effective, but so formal. If you're not interested in learning a discipline, observe the old men and women on their morning walks. Notice how at some times they walk backwards. And how they cup their hands and hit themselves over the arms and chest. After witnessing this the first time, I went home and tried punching myself for a while. It's invigoratingly terrible. Shanghai has some tough old people.

Evening

Okay, so you're more of a nighttime workout person. Well perfect, because that's when things start to get really interesting.

Remember that park with the Tai Chi group? Head back around six or seven in the evening and you'll find a brand new set of old people doing some very light, choreographed dance routines in formation. You probably won't even make it to the park because you'll run into three more crews on your way. Wherever there is space to congregate, you will find grandmothers and grandfathers limbering up to the easy sounds of a nearby boombox. They look like cheerleaders for the world's oldest basketball team.

Sometimes these groups are small and hidden in the entryways of banks and businesses. Sometimes they are made up of dozens of people and have to take to the courtyards of skyscrapers. Whatever the case, they are out there every night no matter the weather. If it's cold, wear your coat. If it's hot, wear your hot-weather pajamas.

There's no need to sign up, because these groups are not organized. One day, somebody brings a boombox to a park and a new class is born. There's no money involved, only love of movement.

That brings us to the final activity of the day. Another dance— an especially good one for you elderly singles out there.

In Xiangyang park, while the evening traffic inches by and the horns blare, people gather together on the stone walkway and it transforms into a ballroom. Someone starts the music, the crowd pairs off, and the makeshift dance floor starts moving. Some of the dancers are phenomenal. Some are just walking in time to the music. But they're all giving their bodies to the rhythm and it's beautiful.

Utility Vest Season

In mid-October, when the city finally has its two to four weeks of fall, old men all over the city start getting giddy. This is their time to shine. They go deep into their closets and pull out the ultimate sign of Shanghainese manliness: the utility vest.

One morning, you'll spot a heavily-pocketed beige number walking down the street. Then you'll turn a corner and see 15,000 more just like it. A sea of fisherman without hats, poles, or anywhere to fish.

Every once in a while you'll come across an adventurous old timer in Olive Drab. And very rare is the sighting of the playboy in a blue so light and powdery, you may go blind just looking at it.

What are they keeping in all those pockets?

Whatever it is, it must be really cool and important, because along with the vests comes a newfound sense of confidence. For those few weeks, these men can declare to their wives: I am capable. I am here to be utilized. If you need me to carry your lip balm, I have the perfectly-sized pocket.

At first, this phenomenon seemed a little silly to me. But then one perfectly clear day as I was walking to the Bund, I came across a meeting of two old men. They shuffled toward each other from the shade of nearby trees and met in the sunlight. Neither said a word, they just smiled, admiring each other's utility vests. Then they unbuttoned them to reveal their arrays of interior pockets. All they did was stand, stare, and smile.

And as I walked away, I kept looking back. It was a few minutes before I had to turn a corner. When I did, they were still standing there.

I am currently shopping for next year's Utility Vest Season.

Black Leather Cap Season

Sure, it's always hard to say goodbye to Utility Vest season, but don't worry, that just means it's time for the Black Leather Caps to come out.

It's the time of year when every man over a certain age suddenly turns into a leather daddy.

And they'll stay that way all winter.

the Taxi

The base price of a taxi is fourteen RMB, which is about $2.25 USD. And if you can keep your trip under three kilometers, it'll stay that way.

It's cheap, and tipping doesn't happen in China so it is in the driver's best interest to get you kinda close to where you want to go as fast as he possibly can.

That's why you are about to go on a roller-coaster ride through the streets of Shanghai. The only difference is on this ride, the danger is real. There are no seatbelts.

Once your driver has put the car in motion, there is no stopping it. He will run bikes off the road, he will pull into oncoming traffic, he will merge into un-merge-into-able lanes. Right turn on red? Yes, without looking or stopping. If he doesn't see you, your safety is not his problem.

I like to think of a Shanghai taxi ride like I think about *Mr. Toad's Wild Ride*. I like to tell myself: "None of this is real. You are having fun. Wow, doesn't that headlight next to your face look realistic? Great craftsmanship!"

Then, when the driver finally gets off of the surface roads and onto the highway, the ride turns into *Space Mountain*. The car speeds up and the flashing LED's covering the buildings are your stars. This is especially true on weekends when the blue lights on the elevated roads are turned on and you can feel yourself travelling into the future.

At this point in the journey, light nausea is normal and expected. There's a good chance that the driver will be smoking through the entire experience, which might not help. But it'll make you just that much happier to reach your destination.

And when you do, consider yourself lucky that you live to cab another day.

Taxi Safe Word

停

TÌNG

"STOP!"

Luxury

Everywhere in Shanghai is a mall.

I mean, the malls are obviously malls, but every other building and even the places that aren't buildings are malls, sort of.

This morning, I woke up and realized I needed coffee filters. The closest supermarket was in a mall. I had to walk past a Gucci store to buy coffee filters.

Across the street from that mall is another mall, and you have to go through that mall to enter the subway.

Then, if you walk about a kilometer down the street, past four other malls and the new mall that is currently under construction, you'll come to an intersection. To cross it, you have to go through yet another mall and walk upstairs to the pedestrian walkway. Once you cross it, you're heading directly toward another, gigantic mall.

Somewhere along the way, China has become obsessed with luxury. I'm no expert, but I guess if you spend a couple decades wearing a tunic, you're bound to want something a little different. That's why my apartment is now five minutes' walking distance from two Prada stores. And why Swarovski teddy bears are readily available at the Pudong Airport, but I have trouble finding a bag of chips.

The city is full of retail. So much retail, I often wonder how only twenty-four million people are going to buy all this stuff.

But it's not just about retail. Everything is in a constant battle to be the fanciest version of itself.

Which KTV (karaoke) are we going to? The one with the anatomically correct horse-shaped disco ball, duh.

Which bar are we going to? The one where little people and circus performers serve you bottles of Dom Perignon with sparklers attached and then dance for you as you drink it, obviously.

There are all kinds of ways to be luxurious in Shanghai, but the ultimate is to own a car. Getting a driver's license in China is easy, but getting a license plate is expensive. There are only so many released every year and, if you want one, you have to bid for it.

Once you have it, you need a car. Very expensive. Never in my life have I seen so many cars that make you say, "Wow, I haven't seen one of those in person before" in one place. You haven't seen them because they're all here. And my favorite part about them is how their owners want them to look.

The day I saw that mirror-finish Maserati, I didn't think any car could be crazier. But then I saw a gold-mirror-finish BMW. Definitely the craziest. But then I saw a baby blue powder-coated Rolls Royce. And finally, I saw a two-tone pink and baby blue powder-coated Rolls Royce. The only logical reason I can imagine for such a car is that it was a gift at the world's most baller baby shower.

From many points of view, Shanghai's love of luxury seems shallow and misdirected. But right now, it makes the city completely singular. Nowhere else in the world will be molded by money into this exact, crazy shape. I can't say if it's good for anyone, and there is no way that it's sustainable, but for now, Shanghai is enjoying the ride.

From my point of view, it means something else entirely. Let's get back to malls for a moment.

When I lived in America, going to the mall was a panic attack in the making. Too many people and too much consumerism, and you're just trying to buy a pair of jeans on sale and Orange Julius is never as good as you remember. But here, going to buy coffee filters next to the Gucci Store has become intensely comforting.

That mall is called iAPM. I think it's name was supposed to stand for International AM and PM because it's supposed to be a late-night mall. You know, in case you needed to buy a Moncler coat at two in the morning.

iAPM is the fanciest mall in Shanghai and maybe all of China. Everything in it is white. It's always immaculately clean and quiet. And it always smells the same, like the fanciest of cleaning products. It led me to write my number-one Shanghai pick-up line:

"Damn girl, you smell like iAPM."

The mall has become a hub for expats like me because it is a completely predictable experience. Suddenly, all these regular people who never set foot inside a Gucci store are piling in just to breathe some fresh air and use a really clean toilet.

We aren't luxurious, but we've learned to love Shanghai's love of luxury.

the Fake Market

Hey, are you into the whole luxury lifestyle thing but don't have the money to support it? Well, you're in luck, everybody else is and nobody else does either. That's why the good people of Shanghai invented the fake market.

A fake market is a multi-level facility filled with tightly packed little stalls selling bootleg versions of name-brand merchandise. Headphones, sneakers, handbags, hats, jackets, dresses, and watches, watches, so many watches.

The proprietors of each stall stand outside and sidle up to you as you pass, offering you the best prices and top brands. Every stall is basically selling the same stuff, so they have to get ahead somehow.

The really smart shops have runners that lock onto you like heat-seeking missiles. They follow you around listing off brand names. Whatever you say you want, don't worry, they have it. Especially if they don't.

But be careful, if you're not sure what you want, they'll just keep following and just keep listing. If you don't say anything, they'll start yelling: "WHAT DO YOU WANT? WHAT DO YOU WANT? WHAT DO YOU WANT" And then you'll be so overwhelmed, you'll start thinking about your life and what you're doing and what is the endgame here anyway? It becomes an intensive therapy session. Eventually, you'll end up yelling back: "I WANT A

CHEAP PAIR OF BEATS BY DRE AND MY FATHER'S APPROVAL!"

When you get home, you'll have made a breakthrough and, after a few days, your new headphones will break as well.

I guess you'll just have to go back to the fake market.

the Marriage Market

On weekends in People's Park, mothers, fathers, grandmothers, and grandfathers take to the stone walkways armed with umbrellas and pieces of paper.

They find a good spot along the path, take a seat, open the umbrellas, and clip their pieces of paper to them.

On those pieces of paper, you will find information about their children or grandchildren. Where they went to school, height, current salary, that kind of thing. All the information that other mothers, fathers, grandmothers, and grandfathers need in order to determine if he or she is a perfect match for their child or grandchild.

This is the Marriage Market. This is where you go when your offspring is further from marriage than you'd like. It's the birthplace of blind dates. Blind dates arranged by your grandmother based on text printed on a sheet of A4.

The Marriage Market is one of the first things you hear about when you come here. I think there are two reasons why every Westerner says you have to see it. And I'm going to give you the second one first:

2. It's beautiful. There's just something about old Shanghainese people tucked away in a park surrounded by lush greenery and umbrellas that makes you feel at peace. Plus, there are huge displays of pink and white paper erected by companies who will show off your offspring for you if you don't feel like hanging around all day. If you can look past all the humanity represented on their pages, they're pretty aesthetically pleasing.

Nearby, there's a little pond where you can see lotus blossom at the right time of year. Next to that, there are public chessboards constantly crowded by old men who have their weekend priorities straight.

And that brings us to the first reason:

1. To Westerners, the whole idea of the Marriage Market sounds like a hilarious nightmare. Why would I let my Mom choose a mate for me based on a sheet of paper that doesn't even have a picture? But at the same time, there's a part of us that would like it to be so easy. We'd love to say:

"I've made a mess of my personal life, would somebody else please figure it out for me? Thanks."

The marriage market represents the dream that somehow, our romantic lives will be sorted out while we sleep in on Saturday.

All laws, no rules

Chinese life is regimented by the government and its liberal use of red tape.

But there are ways to make that tape disappear. I'd like to remain on good terms with the Chinese government, so I won't be specific. I'll just say it usually involves an envelope and the right person. If you put these two things together, anything is possible.

Off-limits suddenly becomes on-limits. You don't really need to worry about riding an illegal scooter if you have a few portraits of Mao handy in your back pocket.

Are you a Westerner who wants to open a business? Well, you're not supposed to, but there are ways around that.

The overhead here is so low, anybody can try any idea. Your bar concept can open its doors in two weeks. There are seamstresses and seamsters ready to execute your fashion label. Your new design firm will have clients from day one. Then if it doesn't work out, you haven't lost your life's savings and you can go on to try the next thing.

In many ways, this is still the wild east. And there's no point in letting a little thing like the law get in your way.

Broken English

Even though this is China, English is everywhere.

You'll see it on signs, on products, on clothes, on bags, and on bootleg DVDs.

Sometimes, the English is perfect. But a lot of times, it's just a little off. And sometimes it's way, way off.

When I first came here, the way off stuff was hilarious. But after a few weeks, it just became part of the experience. There's a woman walking down the street in a shirt that simply says "There's."

Just one word. A contraction, actually. No big deal.

But as you live with it and you see the craziest sentences you've ever seen on a daily basis, the English language begins to change.

New possibilities open up. New ways to expresss emotion. A whole new world of meaning.

The people who are printing these words truly are linguistic pioneers.

To the right, I've recreated a sign I saw over a urinal in a public bathroom. It's my favorite.

Read it. Then wait a few minutes and read it again. Let it sit with you. Wait a week and read it again.

Note your emotional response over time.

This is what I've always wanted talk to you:
URINATING INTO THE POOL YOU ARE THE BEST...

Bikes

My bike is a Phoenix.

It is the classic Shanghai bike.

It's heavy, it's black, and its design hasn't been updated since its release in 1958.

My friend Peter bought it new and left it outside for a year before he sold it to me. It is perfectly rust-covered.

When he handed it off, he said: "Brake early. Actually, start braking when you start pedaling." Good tip.

I asked him if he knew the secret to biking in Shanghai. He did:

"Become a fish."

These are words I've lived by ever since.

There's a flow to the traffic here. If you get hung up on silly things like stoplights and driving the right way down the street, you're going to get yourself hurt. All you have to do is find a place in the pack and worry about the bike directly in front of you. Just match its pace and you'll be fine. If you have death wish, then you can start thinking about passing. Don't worry, you'll get there after a few months.

The vast majority of cyclists in Shanghai are elderly, and they're not afraid to let their age show. They are slow. As slow as possible without tipping over. And believe me, I've seen them test that boundary. I like to say they've got a short way to go and a long time to get there. Not a bad problem to have. Unfortunately, it means that, if there's traffic, you're not going anywhere fast either.

While being a fish will generally keep you safe, there are still many things to watch out for.

Car doors: These are a constant hazard. It doesn't matter if a car is in motion, its doors could open at any time.

Scooters: People who drive scooters aren't overly concerned with which side of the street they should be bombing down. And at night, they aren't overly concerned with using a headlight, so you could be playing a game of chicken and not even know it.

Stopping: Any vehicle or human being can come to a complete halt in the middle of the street at any time. Usually to answer the phone or send a text. They don't care what's happening behind them. If they can't see you, you are not their problem.

Me: My brakes don't work super well. I get them fixed weekly. I'm sorry for running into you in advance.

It's best to keep in mind that bikes are on the bottom of Shanghai's transportation hierarchy. They are cheap and disposable. And if you're on one, so are you.

It goes bus, taxi, car, ambulance, scooter, bike. I guess pedestrian falls at the very bottom, making the fact that ambulance is fourth on the list even more troubling.

If you want to remain alive and have the means, I would recommend traveling inside some kind of motor vehicle. But if you really want to stare death in the face and come out on the other side a changed person, hop on a bike.

Traditionally, when you start making enough money to buy a scooter, you ditch your bike and buy a scooter. When you make enough money to buy a car, you ditch the scooter and buy a car.

I ignored the system entirely. Not only did I buy a bike instead of a scooter, I bought a bike that looks like it belongs to an elderly man with a bad credit history. People don't understand. When my Ayi sees me on it, she squeals with delight. It's like I'm making a joke.

But I do get props from old guys on the street.

And one time, my friend Jimmy, who fact-checked this book, said it was "Very cool."

When I thanked him, he said his grandfather used to have one just like it.

But he has a better one now.

Thanks, Jimmy.

the PHOENIX

the Bund

The Huangpu river flows south from the mouth of the Yangtze. When it hits Shanghai, it bends a few times before heading south again.

The Bund is a stretch of riverfront on the west bank of one of those bends. Before everybody got really excited about communism, it's where all the international banks and trading companies set up their Chinese headquarters. Altogether, they built 52 buildings that look 100 percent out of place in China, and 100 percent of them are still standing.

Today, when you say you're heading to the Bund, it means you're either about to do something very fancy or very touristy.

All the expensive restaurants are over there somewhere, probably in the fanciest hotels. So are the newest, craziest clubs with the newest, bangingest DJs. Places where people are dressed to the nines and the drinks are priced to match.

But across the street is a wide pedestrian walkway that runs north/south along the river. On weekends, when the weather is nice and "the Weather" is okay, it's packed with people enjoying the view of the river, the frankly weird-looking Pearl Tower, and the skyscrapers of Pudong.

At night, the millions of LEDs covering every building illuminate and transform the skyline into a light show. Maybe it sounds a little cheesy, but it's too big not to be cool. Whether you're standing across the river or eating in a restaurant above, it is captivating.

But let's say it's the daytime. Let's say you're standing by the river and think "Man, I'd like to see what's happening on the other side." No problem. You have two options:

Pay three RMB and take the subway across.

or

Pay 50 RMB and take the Bund Sightseeing Tunnel.

I recommend the latter.

The Bund Sightseeing tunnel was conceived as a great glass tube between the shores of the Huangpu. Its creators wanted the public to experience the majesty of the river from the bottom.

Thankfully, at some point along the way, someone had the sense to say: "Wait a minute! This river is gross and brown and filled with trash and the carcasses of farm animals. Why would anyone want to see that?'

They quickly realized their mistake, and plans for a clear tunnel were scrapped. Instead, it seems that the foreman sent an intern to the party store to get some paint, a whole lot of string lights, and a few of those wacky inflatable dancing guys you'd find at a car dealership. They slapped it together over a weekend and opened it to the public.

When you enter, you are packed into a small, glass tram with a bunch of strangers. Then, you move very slowly into the swirling lights of the tunnel. As you go, a pre-recorded voice in the tram tells you what you're seeing. And even though it's speaking both Mandarin and English, it really doesn't make sense at all. First you're under water, then you're surrounded by magma and the voice says: "Paradise and...hell."

So, I guess you're in hell? And then those guys from the car dealership show up.

Well, now that I'm thinking about it, it makes sense.

Then some more lights flash at you and suddenly you're on the other side of the river. Then you can buy another ticket and see the whole thing again in reverse. And all this for only fifteen times the price of the Subway!

I love to make fun of the Sightseeing Tunnel, but I recommend everyone do it once.

I've done it twice.

That, I cannot recommend.

the BUND

RIVER

HUANGPU

the Other Bunds

The Bund is such an iconic part of Shanghai that other stretches of land along the river have started getting jealous.

"Hey, we're bund-shaped, why does that bund get to be THE Bund?"

So now there are two other bunds.

The South Bund

The South Bund is like the actual Bund's teenage brother. It has restaurants, bars, clubs, and museums too, but it feels younger, cooler, and slightly more southern.

The West Bund

The West Bund is my kind of Bund. I first found myself there on a misty winter Friday night. It was early on in my Shanghai residency. I didn't know the area well, so most nights I'd just pick a road and a direction and start walking. That night's road was Wulumuqi, and its direction was south.

Yes, the West Bund is south of the South Bund. Don't ask.

After a while, Wulumuqi Road decided to end. It was dark and barren. No people, no cars. I crossed the final intersection and found a long, wide concrete walkway. When a huge freighter passed into my field of vision, I realized that this was the river.

I walked along the path, under gigantic decommissioned orange container cranes. Leftovers from the Expo, I'd imagine. You'll read more about that later.

During my time there, I only saw one other person. To the east, there was an empty climbing wall and an empty skate park. To the west, there were empty piers; a courtyard with a gigantic LED torch pulsating color, also empty. And a pedestrian underpass that took its design from *2001: A Space Odyssey*. That wasn't empty actually; that was full of dozens of road workers in orange jump suits. They were very surprised to see me.

I'm not sure what their job was supposed to be. If it was sitting around and smoking, they were really earning their keep.

I stood by the water, watched the boat traffic for a while, then walked home, knowing that this, the West Bund, was my place. And if I ever needed to just chill out with some orange dudes or watch some nice boats, it would be there.

That was winter. My next visit to the West Bund happened in spring.

It was packed.

Old ladies were dancing. Old men were singing. Cool young men were playing bike polo on their fixed gears. Nerdy young men were lying down on the concrete, watching television shows on their phones. Kites were flying. I could tell because they all had built-in LEDs that made them stand out against the night sky.

Also because this is China, and we are constantly looking for more things to cover with LEDs.

It was a happening place. One retired man had set up a slackline and was practicing for everyone to see. He even let me try it. I wasn't good. He pointed at me and laughed.

From the slackline, I heard the unmistakable sounds of a sound check. I grabbed my friends and we followed them all the way to the skate park. Yes, there was a free community punk show.

The band was from Beijing. They were very serious about issues. But their adorable drummer didn't get the message. While the lead singer screamed about social reform, her smile was as wide as could be.

The audience was whoever was there anyway. So, the elderly. To my surprise, only a handful got up to leave during the band's first few ear-splitting bars. The rest watched in silence, holding their hands over the ears of their grandchildren. There was polite applause after each song.

All of us there stayed for the entire show. I'm not sure how everyone else felt about it. I guess I was supposed to have been made aware of the troubles of youth in China, but, instead I was charmed yet again by its pajama-clad elderly.

As they moseyed their way home, I thought about the variety of feelings and experiences the West Bund has to offer. I recommend you check it out whenever.

Ghost Cities

It doesn't matter when you're reading this; Shanghai is currently under construction.

That's what they say about every city, right? It's always a new city because the scaffolding is always going up and coming down.

Well, Shanghai is different. It's not just tearing down buildings to put new ones in their places. It's expanding outward. It's creating new cities within the city. And these new cities are huge. Rows upon rows of gigantic, identical apartment buildings as far as the eye can see. Keep in mind that, due to pollution, the eye can't see that far, but it's still impressive.

So they are always building these buildings. Sometimes, though, nobody gets excited about living in them. And sometimes, their funding drops out halfway through construction. That's when Ghost Cities are born.

These are more common the farther you go from the city's center. Take the subway for an hour, get out at a random stop, and start walking. Eventually, you'll find yourself next to a big concrete wall. Jump up and peek over the top and you might see one. Half-finished skyscrapers you'd expect to see in a downtown area, all alone, all dark.

Instead of parking lots, huge tracts of weeds. And probably an army of cats. It's spooky.

But for me, the finished buildings are even spookier. Big, unwanted apartment blocks in the middle of nowhere. It's clear they've sold one unit, because one apartment out of thousands is lit. I think about that person going home every night. Taking the elevator up seventeen floors of emptiness. So alone in the most populous city in the world.

Actually, now that I'm thinking about it, that sounds great. I guess Ghost Cities are a kind of urban rural living experience.

Silence in Shanghai? Sign me up.

Expo 2010

In 2010, Shanghai held the first World Exposition since 1992. They made sure more countries than ever set up pavilions and the attendance was higher than it had ever been before.

The organizers took over huge stretches of both sides of the Huangpu to build the necessary structures. And, in the end, 73 million people showed up to experience pavilions from 246 countries and organizations.

I was not here for the Expo. Sounds exciting; wish I had been.

What I am here for is the aftermath.

Of all those buildings built for the expo, it seems as though only one of them is still in use. And it's in use as a museum about the Expo.

The rest are dark, fenced in, locked up, and guarded 24/7. The grounds aren't cared for, so the plants have taken over.

I first saw them when I was exploring the West Bund on my bike. The air was heavy. The sky was yellow. At one intersection, the sidewalks were filled with people and at the next they had all vanished.

I was alone except for a sanitation worker asleep under a bus shelter, waiting for a bus that would never come. I rode amongst the abandoned modern architecture. Green walls and rooves left to rot. Huge parking structures that would never hold another car.

I had been transported into a dystopian future.

I found myself on Mars in some long forgotten off-world colony. A place that something terrible had made uninhabitable. A concrete wasteland vacated by man and reclaimed by the cats.

My imagination was quickly overtaken by the rational part of my brain.

What are we doing here? Can't somebody use these buildings? Why would you let waterfront property go to waste like this? At the very least, let me take a look around. I'm talking to you, angry man at the gate last week. I'm just trying to experience urban decay, you don't have to yell at me!

Maybe someday, Shanghai will do something with them. But for now, I am confident that if all those cats are drinking out of the Huangpu, they will eventually ingest some kind of chemical that will evolve them into hyper-intelligent beings. In a few thousand years, Expo 2010 will be transformed into a Planet of the Cats situation.

I'm excited for it.

Smells

By stepping outside in Shanghai, you are submitting yourself to a parade of smells.

Honestly, most of them will not be great. You'll quickly learn that the sewers are a little too close for comfort. And the paint used to paint any outdoor surface is so strong that one whiff will leave you lightheaded and a few more will leave you unconscious on the sidewalk.

Some smells are smells that you have never smelled before and probably never will again. Their origin will remain a mystery forever.

The best smells come from food vendors. Sweet things and fried things and barbecued things. But so does the very worst smell of all:

Stinky tofu.

Stinky tofu is a popular street food in Shanghai. It's tofu fermented in brine for several months. I hear it tastes better than it smells, but I guarantee you that I will never get close enough to find out.

The worst part of stinky tofu is it can strike at any time. You'll have no warning. No hint of a stink to tip you off. You'll just walk down the street and all of a sudden, you are fully in the funk. The only thing you can do is cover your nose, run, and hope there isn't another vendor nearby when you run out of breath.

Many people love the smell of stinky tofu. I'd guess that if not the majority, than a large chunk of Chinese people are at least okay with it.

And I envy them.

WAIT! I have an addendum! It is now twenty-four hours after I wrote the above paragraphs and I just walked past a stinky tofu vendor on my corner. I didn't even flinch! I invited it into my nose without realizing and was totally okay with it. It wasn't good, but it was totally ordinary.

This is a big step for me.

Public Restrooms

I love New York City. When I'm there, my favorite thing to do is just walk around. I walk around the park; I walk around the buildings; I walk around absorbing the energy of the city. But it's only a matter of time until a walk around New York City turns into a bathroom emergency.

All of a sudden you're sprinting down the sidewalk, desperately looking for a Starbucks. Or you're walking into random bars, pretending to look for your friends, but actually making a beeline for the men's room.

In Shanghai, that problem doesn't exist. There are public restrooms everywhere.

Shanghai is the only city I've lived in that isn't afraid to talk about our basic human needs. The only city that has taken a step forward and declared:

"We as a people have to go!"

All you need to do is walk down the street and eventually, before the situation gets too intense, you will find one.

The city has even addressed our basic human need of a nice restroom by hiring a full-time janitor to attend each and every one of them.

Sometimes there are both male and female attendants so no restroom will ever have to close for a cleaning.

I can speak only for the men's room, but sometimes these guys stand a little too close while you're peeing. I guess that's just the price you pay for cleanliness.

In all my time here, I have never experienced a bathroom emergency. This means a lot to me.

Thank you, Shanghai.

Public Sleeping

So let's say you're walking down Dongping Lu after a heavy lunch at Di Shui Dong. You yawn, your eyes get heavy, and you think to yourself:

"I could really use a nap. I wonder where I could lie down and shut my eyes for a few minutes."

The answer is: EVERYWHERE!

When the people of Shanghai need to take a nap, they take a nap. No matter where they are. On a park bench, underneath a tree, in the back of a cargo bike, on top of their scooter, or just flat on the concrete somewhere. Feel free to consider the city your bed.

And this isn't just for naptime. In summertime, Lane Houses become little convection ovens. Thanks to no insulation whatsoever, all you can do is sit and sweat. It's especially uncomfortable at night.

Instead, people drag their mattresses out of their homes and onto the sidewalks. There are hundreds of them out in their PJs having a sleeping block party all up and down the street.

The trust these people put in their fellow man is pretty beautiful. They have no worries. They know that they can let their guard down in public for six to eight hours and they'll be totally fine.

It's also pretty beautiful because all of their pajamas are outstanding.

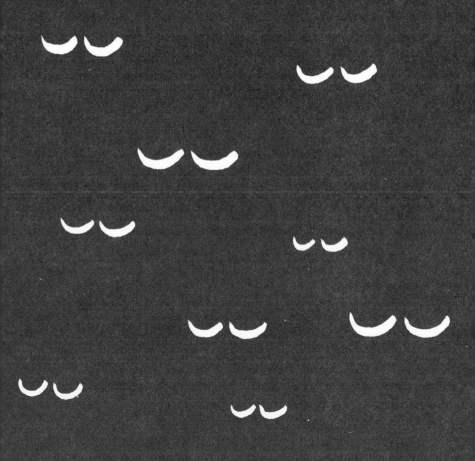

Gongqing

Every park has its green space. This usually consists of heavily manicured lawns surrounded by ropes with signs reading "no step," or something similar.

It's tough to get lost in nature within city limits. I mean, besides overgrown construction sites. It can be tiring and confusing. So much concrete. So much humanity. So little green. And so little oxygen.

So one chilly Saturday, tired of the city and overwhelmed with work, my friend Shaun and I got on the train and headed to a park he had heard about.

It was about an hour from the French Concession. When we got out of the subway, it still looked like Shanghai. Same buildings, same bikes, same no trees. And it was clear from all the stares that this was not a usual Laowai hangout.

After a fifteen-minute walk, we reached the entrance to Gongqing National Forest Park. The entire place was surrounded by brick walls, but we could see the trees popping out over its top, so we went up to the window in the little shack that stood between us and nature. No one was there.

We knocked, but it was only when we yelled "Ni hao" into the emptiness that we heard some shuffling in the back. A woman dressed in black approached the window, held out her hand, and pointed to a sign.

10 RMB.

We paid and walked in. As we passed the back door of the shack, we looked in to find two other women cooking something in a huge pot over a butane stove. The woman who took our money rejoined them, and their eyes followed us down the path.

So we were in the park. And there were trees. And some grass. But we quickly realized that those weren't the things that this park was about. We found a map and it became clear that we weren't in a forest.

We were in an amusement park.

We were the only two people in an amusement park in the middle of winter.

It felt like a ghost town. Except for the fact that as we moved along the path, more and more men dressed all in black would come out from their little shacks and stare at us. And so would the women who sat behind the counters of tiny stands selling snacks, toys, and beer.

We were the only two people in a fully staffed amusement park in the middle of winter.

The carousel man stood by the carousel waiting for someone to ask for a ride. The submarines on the submarine ride had fallen out of favor and into disrepair. The cold war era missile replica with attached zipline was ready to carry some brave soul over the lake.

Just about the only natural thing in Gongqing was a man-made forest that felt like a field of flagpoles with green pipe cleaners taped to them.

No, I guess we wouldn't be getting a natural experience, but at least we could get some good old-fashioned Shanghai weirdness.

As we walked along, trying to get the wild dogs off the scent of our open chip bags, the unmistakable roar of a roller coaster caught our attention. Great idea. We followed the sound to a small kiosk. Inside, we found two men cooking another pot of something over another camp stove. One of the men got up, took another 10 RMB, and ushered us through a rusty gate.

Past some bushes, we found a wooden platform where two men stood next to a roller-coaster car that looked like it had been waiting at the station for a long time.

They called us up the steps, pushed us into the car, and locked us in. Then one of them took the glasses right off my face. I protested, but he wouldn't give them back. That's when I turned around to see the roller coaster itself.

I have very, very bad eyesight. But I didn't need glasses to see the coaster's main feature: a loop.

I was about to be upside down in China. And there was nothing I could do about it.

I am currently alive, so the ride was pretty okay. It was only about 30 seconds long and there was only one moment when I thought the seat belt might give out. I give it three and a-half stars. The man even gave my glasses back.

We knew that if we stayed any longer, we'd be pushing our luck, so it was time to go.

On our way out, we passed the lake. At the lake's edge was a little old man with a pool skimmer, skimming leaves off the water one at a time and very slowly. In the grand scheme of lakes, this was not a huge lake. But it was still a whole lake. This old man's job was to skim an entire lake.

I could not imagine a more sisyphean career. We watched him skim for a while. I thought about the meaning of life. I thought about our neverending quest for purpose. And I thought that the invention of professional lake skimming must be why Shanghai's unemployment rate is so low.

Maybe Gongqing National Forest Park didn't give us the nature we wanted, but we did get a near-death experience and all new levels of existential confusion, which is almost as good.

Fireworks

I'd finished writing this entire book. I headed off to bed and fell asleep knowing that it was ready to be delivered to the publisher.

BOOOOOOOOM!

I woke up to flashes of light and a sound so loud, I could feel it in my chest. By the time I fully understood what was happening, I was cowering in the kitchen. And the first thing I thought was:

"Oh, yeah. You forgot fireworks."

The Chinese invented fireworks, and they've been setting them off like crazy ever since.

You can expect them at any time of the day or night. Usually, you'll hear them on weekend mornings and afternoons. Whenever there's a wedding, whenever a new store opens, or whenever something needs a little good luck. But the real show happens at Chinese New Year.

During CNY, Shanghai is evacuated. Everyone from elsewhere in China goes back to their hometowns to be with family. The expats take a holiday. Work stops, shops close, and the city comes grinding to a halt.

That's when the Shanghainese people start to blow stuff up.

At midnight on the first day of the New Year, the city turns into a war zone.

Non-stop fireworks for a good two hours. And I'm not talking about sparklers. This is professional-grade stuff purchased on the street and ignited by non-professionals. I'm surprised more things don't catch on fire.

Suddenly, you find yourself inside dozens of explosions. And it'll be great. You'll want to live there.

I've had two New Years in Shanghai. The first I spent out on the street, buying and setting off all the fireworks I could afford. The air was thick with smoke and the sky glowed pink. I spent the second on the 39th floor of a nearby hotel. The air was clear. At midnight, I could see the fireworks from miles around. The city was lit up like a birthday cake.

It's not just about the first night, though. The Spring Festival that kicks off the New Year lasts a week. It's not uncommon to hear firecrackers through the days and nights. Finally, just when you thought Shanghai had reached its firework quota for the year, it's the fifth night. The fifth night is the birthday of the god of wealth.

Apparently all of my neighbors really, really, really wanted to get his attention.

Goodbyes

Shanghai has a high turnover rate when it comes to everything. It seems like every week, the street outside my apartment is totally different. Labor is plentiful and inexpensive. You can completely overhaul a storefront in just few days. And you can tear it back down even faster, leaving room for a brand new shop or a brand new restaurant or a brand new pile of rubble.

The same goes for people. I went to a friend's goodbye-drinks last night. I go to a lot of goodbye-drinks. Unless you're Shanghainese, chances are you're not settling in for the long haul.

Shanghai is a stepping stone. It's a waystation even when you're not sure of your destination. I feel it every time I have dinner with my expat friends. All of them are counting down to the day they'll leave and get back to their normal lives.

This is not an easy place to be. It's endlessly fascinating, but never quite comfortable. Sometimes you can get bogged down in that discomfort and lose track of how important it is to not be normal for a while. To see what life means away from home. To hang out with twenty-four million people who see the world in a different way. And whose priorities are totally different than your own.

This city has given me more perspective on the human experience than I thought I'd ever have. And as embarassing as it is, it has taught me the meaning of "cultural differences."

I know I'll leave someday, and it's easy to convince myself that when I do, I won't miss it. The air is bad, you can't drink the water, it's crowded, and it's noisy. But I will miss Shanghai.

It's easiest to realize when I have jet lag. I wake up at four in the morning and can't get back to sleep, so I go outside and walk. The streets are empty except for a few packs of club hoppers having a breakfast of noodles and Tsingtao on the sidewalk. A few elderly people are heading to the park for their morning exercise. The light is beautiful. It's quiet. It's nice. That's when I know for sure that this is a magical place.

But just now I took a shower and the hot water broke immediately.

Oh, Shanghai.

谢谢

XIÈ XIÈ

Thank You